Like our Facebook page
@RiddlesandGiggles

Follow us on Instagram
@RiddlesandGiggles_Official

Questions & Customer Service
hello@riddlesandgiggles.com

Halloween Joke Book for Kids

by Riddles and Giggles™

www.riddlesandgiggles.com

D1304450

FREE BONUS

Get your FREE book download

*Halloween Jokes &
Would You Rather for Kids*

- ⊘ Contains a collection of fang-tastic Halloween Jokes and Would You Rather Halloween-Themed Questions
- ⊘ More endless giggles and entertainment for the whole family.

**Claim your FREE book at
www.riddlesandagiggles.com/halloween**

Or scan with your phone to get your free download

TABLE OF CONTENTS

WELCOME

Hi there, Jokester!

Jokes are a great way for people to have fun and share laughs together.

Lots of people love to tell jokes. Some are very funny. Some are just corny. Other jokes make no sense at all. One thing we can agree on about jokes is that kids love them!

I hope you are one of those kids, because if you want a collection of funny, corny, and laugh-out-loud jokes, this book is for you!

The *Halloween Joke Book for Kids* is an awesome collection of good, clean, fun jokes that will make you roll your eyes, snort, giggle, groan, and laugh out loud.

You can read this whole book or pick which jokes you want to read in any order you want.

You can also enjoy reading the jokes on your own, or share the jokes with everyone around you. You can also take turns reading the jokes out loud with family and friends.

Use these jokes when trick-or-treating and just maybe you'll get an extra treat or two!

So, grab your Halloween treats and have fun enjoying these Halloween jokes.

PSST...You can also color in the Halloween pictures and use this book as a coloring book AND a joke book!

TIPS ON HOW TO TELL A JOKE

- ⊘ Practice reading the joke out loud a few times to help you remember it. You may want to practice reading in front of a mirror.

- ⊘ Find a family member or friend and ask them if they want to hear a joke.

- ⊘ As you tell the joke, remember to say it slowly and clearly so people understand every word.

- ⊘ Adding a small pause helps to build up suspense and can make the joke even funnier.

- ⊘ Deliver the final punch line. Remember to say it slowly, then wait for the laughs.

- ⊘ If you mess up, that's OK. Move on and tell another joke. Remember, everyone loves jokes!

1

PUMPKINS & JACK-O'-LANTERNS

What do you call a mean pumpkin?
A Jerk-o'-Lantern.

Where does a pumpkin go to get a good cleaning?
The car-ve wash.

What kind of light is inside a Jack-o'-Lantern?
Candlefright.

Why did the pumpkin need glasses?

So it can see-d.

What do Jack-o'-Lanterns say to
each other on Halloween?

"Happy hollow ween!"

What did one pumpkin say to another?

Orange you glad we're not carved yet?

Why did the vampire sit on the pumpkin?

It wanted to play squash.

What do you call a hillbilly Jack-o'-Lantern?
A country pumpkin.

What do you get when you cross a pumpkin and Bigfoot?
Sasquash.

How do Jack-o'-Lanterns know all the latest gossip?
They hear it through the pumpkin vine.

What is professional pumpkin wrestling called?
Smack-o-Lantern.

How do you mend a broken Jack-o'-Lantern?

With a pumpkin patch.

What's the best workout for a Jack-o'-Lantern?

Pumpkin iron.

How do you know if a pumpkin is not a good pick?

If it looks a little seedy.

What do you call a large Jack-o'-Lantern?

A plumpkin.

What's a Jack-o'-Lantern's favorite way to listen to music?

Vine-yl records.

What did the pumpkin say to the kids?
Cut it out.

What's a pumpkin's favorite movie?
Pulp Fiction.

What do you call a group of pumpkin besties?
#SquashGoals

What do you call a pumpkin that's
had a little too much carving?
A Jack-oww-Lantern.

Why are Jack-o'-Lantern's so forgetful?
Because they're empty headed.

2

WITCHES & VAMPIRES

Why did the vampire give his girlfriend a blood test?
To see if she was his blood type.

What happened to the naughty witch at school?
She was ex-spelled.

Which famous sites does Dracula like to visit?
The Vampire State Building and Count Rushmore.

Why did the witch have to sit down?
She had a dizzy spell.

Which story do all little witches love to hear at bedtime?
"Ghoul Deluxe and the Three Scares."

Why do people hate being bitten by vampires?
Because it's a drain in the neck

Why won't a witch wear a flat hat?
Because there's no point in it.

Why did the vampire take up acting?
It was in his blood.

Which vampire ate the three bears porridge?
Ghouldilocks

What is a vampire's favorite flavor of ice cream?
VEINilla.

How does a witch travel when she doesn't have a broom?
She witch hikes.

What do little vampires get in their snack lunches?
Blood oranges.

Why do witches make great authors?
They know how to write spell-binding stories.

HALLOWEEN JOKE BOOK FOR KIDS

What is a vampire's favorite fruit?

Adam's apples and neck-tarines.

What sort of group do vampires join?

A blood group.

Why did the team of witches lose the baseball game?

Their bats flew away.

What's a vampire's favorite after school activity?

Going to the batting cages.

What breed of dog do vampires have?

Bloodhound.

What's the problem with twin witches?

You can never tell which witch is witch.

What did the mommy vampire say to the little vampire?

"You're driving me batty."

What is the first thing that vampires learn at school?

The Alphabat.

Where did the vampire open up his savings account?

At a blood bank.

How does a vampire like his food served?

In bite sized pieces.

What do you call a witch's garage?

A broom closet.

Why are vampires like false teeth?
They all come out at night.

What's a witch's favorite bug?
A spelling bee.

Why are vampire families so close?
Because blood is thicker than water

What do you call an Alaskan vampire?
Frostbite.

What noise was the witch's car making when she started it up?

BROOM BROOM.

What's it called when a witch's cat falls off a broomstick?

A cat-asprophe.

What do you call a vampire that can't stop eating Halloween candy?

Count Snackula.

Why was the vampire marathon race too close to call?

It finished neck and neck.

Why don't witches like to ride on their brooms when they're angry?

They're afraid of flying off the handle.

What type of coffee do
vampires prefer?

Decoffinated.

What do witches use in their hair?

Scare-spray.

How does a warlock ask
a witch to dance?

"Voodoo like to dance with me."

What's a vampire's favorite sport?

Batminton.

What do witches and candles
have in common?

They're both wicked.

Why did the vampire get fired from the blood bank?
He was caught drinking on the job.

What was the witch's favorite subject in grade school?
Spelling, of course.

What do you call a confused witch?
Perp-hexed.

What favorite test do vampires love to take?
A blood test.

What do witches say when they overtake each other?
Broom, broom, broom.

How does a witch
like her coffee?

With a little scream
and sugar.

Why did the witch give
up fortune telling?

She didn't see any
future in it.

What did the skeleton
say to the vampire?

You suck.

Why did the witch put
her boom in the wash?

She wanted a
clean sweep.

What is the vampire's
favorite slogan?

Please Give Blood
Generously.

What does a warlock say to his witch bride when they're getting married?

"I'll take you for witcher or poorer."

How many vampires does it take to change a light bulb?

None, vampires like the dark.

What does a vampire take for a bad cold?

Coffin drops.

Why do witches get good bargains?

Because they love to haggle.

What happened when a boy vampire met a girl vampire?

It was love at first bite.

HALLOWEEN JOKE BOOK FOR KIDS

Why was everyone avoiding the vampire?

They had bat breath.

What kind of tests do they give in witch school?

Hex-aminations.

Where do vampires prefer to go to eat lunch?

A Casketeria.

Why did the vampire go to the hospital?

He wanted his ghoulstones removed.

Why was the witch late for the Halloween party?

She lost her witch-watch.

GHOSTS, MONSTERS & ZOMBIES

What did the monster say when their friend
arrived late to the Halloween party?

"It's about Frankentime."

What's a werewolf's favorite holiday?

Howl-oween.

What do you call a monster with a stuffy nose?

The boogerman.

What does a ghost with allergies sound like?
Ahh...ahh...ahhBOOOO.

Why can ghosts never get away with telling a lie?
You can see right through them.

Why did the ghost need a tissue?
He had too many boo-gers.

What's a monster's favorite pie?
Key slime pie.

What trees do ghouls like best?
Ceme-trees.

What did the baby ghost eat for lunch?

A boo-loney sandwich.

What do you call a monster who can't
stop playing jokes on their friends?

Prankenstein.

Why does Frankenstein laugh the hardest at corny jokes?

He's always in stitches.

HALLOWEEN JOKE BOOK FOR KIDS

How do you greet a three-headed monster?

Hello, hello, and hello.

What do you call a monster with no neck?

The Lost Neck Monster.

Where does a ghost go on vacation?

Mali-boo.

What did the monster do when he lost his hand?

He went to the second-hand shop.

What do monsters eat for lunch at Monster School?

Human beans, boiled legs, pickled
bunions and eyes-cream.

Why are ghost parties so dull?

Because no one can be the life of the party.

Why was the big, scary, two-headed
monster top of the class at school?

Because two heads are better than one.

What is a monster's favorite food?

Ghoul scout cookies.

How does a monster count to 31?

On his fingers.

What position does a monster
play on the soccer team?

Ghoulie.

What kind of streets do zombies like to haunt?

Dead end streets.

What's the first thing ghosts do
when they get in a car?

They boo-kle their seatbelts.

Where do zombies go for cruises?
The Deaditerranean.

What do ghosts like to eat for dinner?
Spook-ghetti.

What did the zombie get his medal for?
Deadication.

What games do little ghosts like to play?
Corpse and robbers, peek-a-boo, and hide-and-go-shriek.

How did the ghost say goodbye to the vampire?
So long sucker.

What's a ghoul's favorite breakfast cereal?
Rice Creepies.

What do little zombies play?
Corpses and Robbers.

How do you know a zombie is tired?
He's dead on his feet.

What do ghosts dance to?
Soul music.

HALLOWEEN JOKE BOOK FOR KIDS

4

SKELETONS & SKULLS

What do skeletons say
before eating dinner?

Bone appetit.

What do skeletons use
to make s'mores?

Marsh-marrows.

How can skeletons tell
when it's going to rain. They
feel it in their bones.

What art form are
skeletons best at?

Skull-pture.

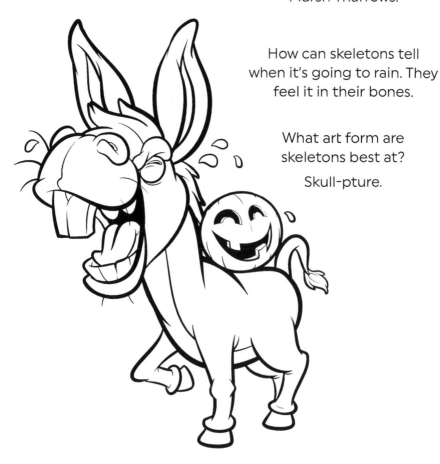

What did the skeleton say while losing a card game?

"I have no skin in this game."

How do skeletons say goodbye?

See you to-marrow.

What forms of major education do skeletons attend?

High Skull.

What's a skeleton's good luck charm?

A wishbone.

Why did the skeleton go to the party?

For a rattling good time.

What type of art do skeletons like?

Skull tures.

What do you call a flying skeleton?

A bone drone.

What did the skeleton think of their surprise Halloween party?

They were bone away.

Where do skeletons go to work?

In giant skullscrapers

What do you call a lonely skeleton?

A no body.

What do you call a skeleton who can't stop taking naps?

Lazy bones.

Why do skeletons
hate winter?

Because the cold goes
right through them.

Why don't skeletons
like to eat spicy food?

They can't stomach it.

When does a
skeleton laugh?

When something
tickles his funny bone.

How do French
skeletons say hello?

Bone-jour.

What did the skeleton
say while riding his
motorcycle?

I'm bone to be wild.

Why are skeletons
usually so calm?

Nothing gets
under their skin.

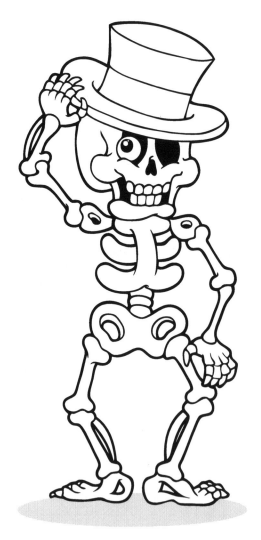

What does a skeleton order at a restaurant?

Spare ribs.

What do you call a young skeleton?

A skele-teen.

What kind of plate does a skeleton eat off?

Bone china.

5

BATS, CATS & CREEPY CRAWLIES

What are horses called
on Halloween?

Night mares.

What do you call a black cat
that eats too many lemons?

A sourpuss.

What Halloween animal
is best at gymnastics?

An acro-bat.

What's a spider's favorite
thing to do on a computer?

Make websites.

What do you call black cats
walking together on Halloween?

A purr-ade.

What do black cats say
when they get mad?

"You've gotta be kitten me."

What do you call a bat who's
stuck inside a bell?

A dingbat.

What do you call a witch's cat that
never comes when he's called?

Impussible.

What does Dracula say when he
doesn't have good news?

"I have BAT news, everyone."

What did the black cat say to
their friend who didn't get much
candy trick-or-treating?

"Stay pawsitive."

What subject are black cats best at in school?

Hisstory.

What do you call
two spiders on their
honeymoon?

Newlywebs.

What's it called when
black cats accidentally
show up in the same
Halloween costume?

Copycats.

What's a bat's
favorite dessert?

Pineapple
upside-down cake.

What does a spider's
bride wear?

A webbing dress.

Why did no one eat what the
cat brought to the party?

It was really clawful.

What do black cats do when
they can't solve a problem?

They start from scratch.

Why do bats make great friends?

They love to hang out.

What event do spiders love to attend?

Webbings.

Why did the spider buy a car?

So he could take it out for a spin.

What did the spider do when
he went on his computer?

He visited his web site.

What did the bat say
to his girlfriend?

You're fun to hang around with.

Why did the witch feed
her cat with pennies?

She wanted to put some
money in the kitty.

What kind of bird is
the spookiest?

A scare-crow.

What's a spider's
favorite workout?

Spin class.

6

HAUNTED HOUSES & GRAVEYARDS

How did you know that
house was haunted?

It was at the dead
end of the street.

What do you call a haunted
house that's a fixer-upper?

It just has some
wear and scare.

What do you use to
unlock the front door
of a haunted house?

A spoo-key.

What's the safest place
in a haunted house?

The living room.

What's the best time of day
to visit a haunted house?

Early in the mourning.

What do cemetery workers and baseball players have in common?

They take their breaks in a dugout.

What did the cookie and the haunted house have in common?

They were both crumbling.

Why did the trick-or-treater leave the haunted house party?

They were eerie-tated.

Why are graveyards so noisy?
Because of all the coffin.

What hotel do werewolves stay at?
The Howliday Inn.

7

TRICK-OR-TREATING & HALLOWEEN FUN

What do pandas get for trick-or-treating?

Bam-boo.

What do you call a sucker who can't stop laughing?

A LOLipop.

What do you say before someone leaves to go trick-or-treating?

"Be scareful out there."

What do you call the winner of the best costume contest?

Hallowqueen.

What do puppies say on Halloween?

"Lick or treat."

What do birds say on Halloween?

"Trick or tweet."

HALLOWEEN JOKE BOOK FOR KIDS

What kind of nightmares do candy bars have?

None, they only have sweet dreams.

If you're dressed as a cheetah, what do you say on Halloween?

"Quick or treat."

If you're dressed as a construction builder, what do you say on Halloween?

"Brick or treat."

What do you call a farmer in costume?

Jolly rancher.

What do you call a lawyer in costume?

A law suit.

How do you trick-or-treat at a monster's house?

Ring the roar bell.

What's the best day of the week for
eating all your Halloween candy?

Chewsday.

What should you do if you find yourself in the
same room as Frankenstein, Dracula, a werewolf,
a vampire and a coven of witches?

Keep your fingers crossed that it's a
fancy dress Halloween party.

Why did the peanut butter cup quit its job?
It wasn't very ful-filling.

What do you call french fries on Halloween?
Terrorfries.

What's the best soup to serve at Halloween dinner?
Alpha-bat soup.

What's the best candy for recess?
Monkey bars.

What's the best Halloween game to
play at a friend's house?

Hide and shriek.

What's the most fun Halloween carnival ride?

Scary-go-round.

What's the best way to watch Halloween movies?

On a big scream TV.

What makes eggs such a great Halloween dinner?
They're terrorfried.

What's the best entree for Halloween dinner?
Spooketti and meatballs.

What's a police officer's favorite candy?
Lollicops.

What do you call a chimpanzee that ate
too much Halloween candy?

A chunky monkey.

What do you call parents that are
really excited for Halloween?

Mummies and deadys.

What Halloween party game are mummies the worst at?

Twister...they get tangled.

8

ONE-LINERS

Vampires will fall for anything.
They're real suckers.

You can't miss the cemetery.
It's a dead giveaway.

The house down the street is so haunted
even the windows have shudders.

Do you know if that vampire is okay?
I thought I heard him coffin.

The cemetery down the street is almost full. People are dying to get in there.

The haunted house finally sold. I guess someone found it eerie-sistable.

A local farmer thought his chicken coop was haunted. He had to call the eggs-ocist.

I heard two witches telling jokes. Broom broom.

Fangs for the memories.

You're just my (blood) type.

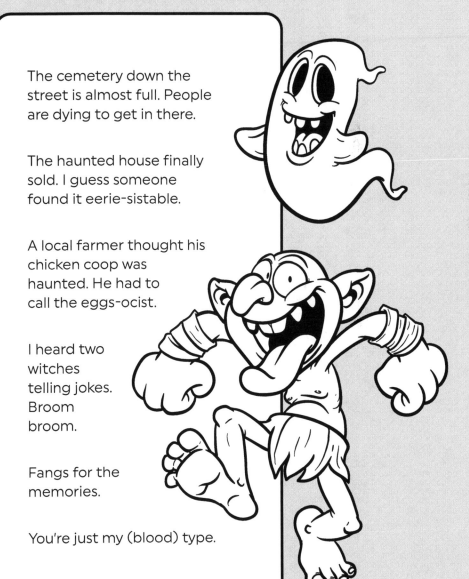

BEFORE YOU GO

Did you have fun with those sometimes corny, Halloween jokes?

Now that you have gotten the hang of jokes, spend some time thinking up some of your own! Create your own jokes about fun things you like to do.

For Halloween, you can create jokes about witches, ghosts, monsters, zombies, haunted houses and the fun you can have during Halloween such as costumes, parties and not to mention trick-or-treating.

Once you think up your own jokes, you can play the game anywhere! It is a great game to play on long road trips, at school, or even when you are waiting in line at the grocery store.

Have fun coming up with your own jokes and endless giggles!

WRITE YOUR OWN JOKES!

Have fun coming up with your own jokes and endless giggles!

BenyU

HALLOWEEN JOKE BOOK FOR KIDS

HALLOWEEN JOKE BOOK FOR KIDS

HALLOWEEN JOKE BOOK FOR KIDS

HALLOWEEN JOKE BOOK FOR KIDS

HALLOWEEN JOKE BOOK FOR KIDS

HALLOWEEN JOKE BOOK FOR KIDS

COLLECT THEM ALL!

| Halloween Would You Rather for Kids | Halloween Joke Book for Kids | Halloween Knock Knock Joke Book for Kids |

www.riddlesandgiggles.com

REFERENCES

41 Hilarious Monster Jokes And Puns That Are Dead Funny! (n.d.). Laffgaff.com. https://laffgaff.com/monster-jokes-puns/

Liles, M. (2020, September 26). *75 Funny Halloween Puns That'll Get All the Guys and Ghouls Howling.* Parade. https://parade.com/1059333/marynliles/halloween-puns/

Munden, E. (2020 10). *60 Vampire Puns That Are Bitingly Funny.* Kidadl Ltd. https://kidadl.com/articles/vampire-puns-that-are-bitingly-funny

O'Sullivan, K., & Donovan, B. (2021, June 22). *70 Funny Halloween Puns That'll Give All Your Ghoul Friends a Good Cackle.* Country Living; Hearst. https://www.countryliving.com/life/a23012541/halloween-puns-funny-cute/

Schaulis, M. (2017, December 21). *35 Puns That Will Make Your Day.* Kettle Fire Creative. https://kettlefirecreative.com/puns/

Made in the USA
Las Vegas, NV
10 October 2021

32102969R00057